RONDA

BY

JOSE PAEZ CARRASCOSA

COLLABORATIONS
TRANSLATION BY MRS. GRACE ROGERS

PROLOGUE: D. Gonzalo Huesa Lope

PICTURES: D. J. Agustín Núñez - Edilux

DRAWINGS: D. Cayetano Arroyo

My sincere thanks
to everyone.
THE AUTHOR

7th Edition, 2010.

PUBLICACIONES RONDA 2000
C/ INFANTE N° 67
ISBN: 84-604-6022-3
DEPÓSITO LEGAL: GR-617-1995
FOTOMECÁNICA: Franacolor, S.L.
IMPRIME: Copartgraf (Granada)

DEDICATED
To my dear wife and children

PROLOGUE

It certainly is not easy to convert something simple, or feasible into something outstandig, or something manageable into something grandiose. Nevertheless dear reader, this is to my mind, the great feature of the book which you are about to read. The beautiful complexity of nature, history and art, which Ronda encompasses, the extraordinary richness of its landmarks which ecology and human works have progressively imposed on her, all this the author has set out in a simple, feasible and manageable form.

You will have heard and read a great deal about this enchanting town because there has been much varied and erudite matter written and spoken about her. She deserves it. Her enviable site in the centre of the mountains of the Serrania, her inaccessibility and isolation, her response to light and limpidity and the allure of the sun at dawn or the spring and autumnal sunsets, the noble sobriety of her monuments, all this has contributed to the making of legends which enhance this city created for dreaming, for enjoyment and to live in. The author knows this and wishes to offer you something exceptional and different. He does not wish you to read. He does not wish tou to speak. Neither does he wish you to listen. He wishes you to take part in a dialogue; he does not wish you to be dumb, he wishes you to converse. This is what it is all about; that you should not be just a passive reader of what is said, but you should become his fellow traveller, agreeable and loquatious during your visit to the city of wonders.

This book contains authentic history, the charm of legends, and the warm caress of sensibility in the face of its beauty. You will find the author's style, and his words familiar, cordial and colloquial just as if you were walking through yout own home town. Full of affection and friendship. Read and you will find that you have acquired a new friend with whom you can comverse of noble and agreeable themes. This is what I would wish for you that your dialogue should be lively, pleasent and charming. This will be your unforgettable visit to Ronda. Happy reader.

Gonzalo Huesa Lope.

⇦ **Foto Kurt Hielscher - 1918**

Vicente Espinel. Picture by Cuso

INTRODUCTION

I, sir, am from Ronda, queen and lady of the Serrania, protected by her monuntains and summits just like a spoilt child by God's will. Situated on a plateau at 780 metres in the south west of Malaga province, she watches over and protects us, being a natural and the most impregnable fortress in this part of Spain.

– The most impregnable?

Don't you believe me? well then, come with me to our bridge and, from it you will realise the truth of what I am saying and also the beauty which up till now you have missed.

Look over there, where the sun is setting, can you see those blue peaks? Well, those are the Sierra de San Cristobal and the Sierra de Grazalema, the first thing that he, who comes from America by boat, sees, They rise to a height of 1.640 metres, and they have the highest rainfall of the whole peninsula. Now a nature reserve for Pinsapos and Wild Animals.

But don't let your eyes stray; look to the left. That is the Sierra Perdiguera; that is where the road to Algeciras passes towards Gibraltar, the land of smugglers and highwaymen, wounded hearts and lost hopes.

What are you telling me? that you have never heard of the smugglers and bandits of Ronda? But, wherever have you been all this time? have you never heard of José María the 'Tempranillo' or the 'Pasos Largos'? Well listen. There are still people in Ronda who can tell you of the times when they have gone to a certain place and have returned loaded to Ronda and they could also tell you that to ride to Gibraltar on a horse was just a pleasant outing; with a good guide and getting up very early, it was a ten hour ride, and, after a light lunch and a rest in La Linea, the return trip and arrival at dawn in Ronda.

But do not linger. Come to the other side of the bridge where the sun is showing us its first rays. Have you never seen a sunrise or a sunset in Ronda? Pity! you don't know what you have lost! but don't worry that is easily remedied...

Look, those are the Sierras of Melequetin, Hidalga, Oreganal, and the Sierra de las Nieves. That is the highest point in the province of Malaga, the Torreccilla, 1.919 metres high.

On clear days, from that point one can see the whole of the Costa del Sol.

In the Sierra de las Nieves there is a kind of tree called Pinsapo Abies, Boissier a botanical species exclusive only to this place and to the Urals, in Russia, although there are a few examples in the Sierra de Gredos, near Madrid.

– You are right I have heard it said that it is a plant from the tertiary era.

Now look down. Well? wonderful don't you think?

Friend, there is nothing more beautiful than this Gorge with its river Guadalevin at the bottom, clinging to its banks through which an impetuous stream flows in winter.

– What does Guadalevin mean?

It really means 'The deep river', though other versions translate it as 'Milk river'.

– Has the river been carved out the Gorge?

Well, up to a point. The gorge has been formed by river erosion: The difference in the hardness of the rock, formed by tertiary sediments whose conglomerates and sandy stratas of miocene elements have carved out the steep beauties of al Wadi-al-laban gorge.

There is quite a flow in the river which increases greatly when it rains for it has its source in the Sierra de las Nieves and near Ronda it picks up water from the streams la Toma and Las Culebras; further down the valley it joins the river Alcobacin and later continues its flow in the river Guadiaro.

– In winter. It's quite frightening to pass over the bridge, isn't it?

I should think it is cold in winter and how! You are right, in winter it is cold and it snows on the mountains; but our climate is extremely healthy and, besides the winter is short. But, what do you think of the summer?

The summers are marvellous. Yes, it is hot some days in August; but when the sun sets the temperature is so agreeable that it makes one forget the few hours of heat which after all, is what one expects of summer.

In any case it is a dry heat and Ronda is about the most healthy place you could find: without any contamination or anything worrying and besides with springs and autumns that are the envy of many people.

– And what does Ronda live on?

Ronda as the principal town of the Serrania and its commercial centre; it has a selection of shops that are as good in quality, in price as any that can be found in bigger towns.

It counts on the elaboration of pork products, its chorizo and hams being world famous.

The making of Castilian crafted furniture is very important, it is made of quality woods such as chestnut or walnut.

Today several factories have been started for the making of cheese from the rich goat's milk and ewe's milk of our serrania and also a few factories that turn out confectionery and tiles.

Finally, agriculture completes the list of its resources.

– Tell me, why did you say that Ronda was an impregnable town?

Do not be too formal in Ronda everybody is a friend.

You will tell me whether it is impregnable or not.

On its northern side there is the gorge of 100 metres in height; on the park side it is 170 metres high: on the west the same characteristics apply and precipices which united to the ramparts continue to the Alcazaba to the south. There are the principal gates into Ronda; the Almocábar gate and the Charles I gate. The first one is from the XIIIth. century and gave access to the Alcazaba and the second built in the XVIth. century has the arms of the House of Austria over it.

These gates gave access to the Alcazaba of Ronda and were well fortified because this southern side is the only natural access to the city. Then on the eastern side double ramparts continue to the gates Exijara and Phillip V and then continue again to the Tajo.

What do you say about the fortifications of the city of Ronda? Was it really inaccessable?

– A city like this will have a rich history won't it?

It has, and a great part of it has taken place on its ramparts and houses. But allow me first to give you a general outline. Then you will accompany me around corners and through squares and doors and along streets past the grills and shadows whose stones revive 3000 years of history.

Aniya la Gitana.- painting by Miguel Martín

A BRIEF HISTORY
Concerning the very noble and
loyal town of Ronda

The origins of the city of Ronda go back to the Bastulo Celts, who called it Arunda, although their lands had formerly been inhabited by prehistoric man; their megalithic monuments such as "Los Arenosos" and the cave of "La Pileta", with its paleolithic paintings and neolithic ceramics prove this, or the recent excavations in the old town which confirm continuous habitation from Neolithic times to our own era.

Ronda had very few commercial ties with the Phoenicians because the latter on their arrival in our land, found near Arunda a village of iberian origin called Acinipo. There they settled and improved the existing constructions. For them this was an ideal situation in view of their commercial aspirations with the interior of the country and because Acinipo is situated at the same distance from Malaga and Cadiz, both Phoenician colonies.

The Greeks skirted our Serrania searching for routes for their traffic with the Tartessos and also to distance themselves from Punic influence.

Arunda became a Greek colony named Runda.

– And could you tell me what Arunda and Acinipo mean?

Well, Arunda means "Surrounded by Mountains", and Acinipo means "The Land of Wine".

In the second century B.C. the Romans entered the peninsula and expelled the Carthaginians. Immediately our town, taking advantage of its situation, is converted into a fortress in which the Castle of Laurel was built. Acinipo was converted into a town, becoming a municipality with powers to mint money and later on its citizens acquired the same rights as any citizen of imperial Rome.

Sertorius, in his war against Pompey, destroyed Runda, and changed its name to Munda.

In the year 45 B.C. a pagan temple was built commemorating the victory of Caius Julius Ceasar over Cneus and Sextus the sons of Pompey. We will speak about this temple on our visit to Sta. Maria. So the Roman domination continues and the natives on their side assimilate their culture and customs, but maintaining their natural location and priviledged situation near the Roman crossroads coming from Cadiz via Zahara, and from Gibraltar through the Guadiara valley towards El Burgo and Iluro.

With the invasion of the Sueves, the Vandals and the Alani and still later the Visigoths both Munda and Acinipo were destroyed and plundered. But the Gothic king Atanagildo begs the Bizantine Emperor Justinian for help against the Agili. The latter is rewarded with the south eastern coast of Spain, creating the province of Orospeda which included Ronda.

The Bizantine Greeks seek the lands where their ancestors had possessed Runda. They discovered the ruins of Acinipo and Runda and realised that the former were in better condition and also its situation pleased them more, so they installed themselves in it and they called it Runda; the township would be regained again by the Visigoths during the time of Suintila.

For this reason Acinipo is called Ronda la Vieja (Old Ronda).

It is after the year 711 under Arab domination that Ronda takes up its place in the history of Spain, becoming one of the most important towns and fortresses in the south of Spain.

When our country was invaded the ruins of the castle of Laurel and the city of Munda were found. it was decided to build a town on these ruins which would be called Izna-Rand-Onda, the city of the castle, the chief point of communication and union of the Caliphate with the African territories.

Under the rule of Omeya, Ronda became the capital of a Waliato or Kura a province with the name of Tacoronna, which comprised all of this mountainous region, changing from being a simple castle into a large town.

In this epoch important buildings were raised such as mosques, palaces etc:, the walls were strengthened as well as its defenses. In the south wall the main door was opened, called the door of Almocabar, and in the east wall that of Exijara, joining the old suburbs to the 'Medina' (market).

Umar-Ben-Hafsun was born in 854 near our town in the village of Parauta.

Of noble Gothic Christian origen he fomented unrest from 899 to 917 under the rule of the Omeyas.

Taking advantage of christian discontent on account of Moslem abuses, he placed himself at the head of a large mozarabic army rising in rebellion against the Moslem troops and maintaining dominion over large regions of the south of Spain.

He chose as his headquarters a place named Bobastro, situated between the valleys of Abdalagis, Ardales and Alora here in the province of Malaga.

The courage and fame of this man from Ronda became more and more well known, numerous volunteers, desiring liberty and independence for their lives, religion and lands joined him.

The war was continued for ten years by the descendants of Umar-Ben-Hafsun until they were defeated by the Caliph of Cordoba, Who totally destroyed the work of Umar.

The attempts of Umar to obtain the independence of our land is praiseworthy as he had managed to dominate the whole of the province of Malaga; part of that of Cadiz with Algeciras, part of the provinces of Granada and Almeria, even advancing against the province of Cordoba and capturing the town of Cabra on his way towards the capital of the caliphate.

With the disappearance of the caliphate of Cordoba at the beginning of the 11th. century the kingdoms of the Taifas appear on the scene.

Ronda becomes, under the Berber dynasty of the Banu-Ifran the capital of one of them, ruled by Abu-Nur who governs in peace and prosperity for 39 years.

New villages are born in its 'Serrania' and its buildings and industry improve.

During this period the kingdom of Ronda is coveted both by the kings of Malaga and of Sevilla. The latter, Mothadir of Sevilla murders Abu-Nasir, son and successor of Abur-Nur, at a banquet. The king of Ronda being dead, Mothadir incorporates into the kingdom of Sevilla the kingdom of Inza-Rand and all its territories in the year 1059.

With the invasión of the Almoravides (warrimg tribes from the Atlas) the name of our town Izna-Rand is changed into that of Madinat Runda and continues to be ruled by them for 71 years until they are expelled by the Almohades.

During the domination of these Madinat Runda sometimes belongs to Africa and at others to the kingdom of Granada, changing allies and enemies with extraordinary facility, until finally the Almohades are defeated at the battle of Navas de Tolosa.

The chronicles of Castile narrate that during this epoch the moors of Ronda were the most intrepid and courageous in this land of the moors.

Alfonso XI relates how he destroyed lands, and vineyards in Ronda, Antequera and Archidona hoping to weaken his enemies through lack of food.

The king of Castile fought for four days in this campaign in our land but had to abandon it for lack of provisions.

In the year 1314 the king of Granada Ismail III frightened by the advance of the Christian forces under Alfonso XI seeks help from the African Benimerines, this is granted by the sultan of Morocco Abul Hassan, who sends his son Abomelic.

This latter having arrived declares himself King of Ronda, Algeciras and Gibraltar, making Ronda the capital of his dominions.

At this time prosperity and splendour comes to our town. There are important constructions such as the bridge in the old suburb or the stairs in the rock with 360 steps built into the live rock which supplied the town water from the bottom of the gorge, or the mills supplying oil and flour for the town.

Abomelic was killed in the battle of Alberito by the troops of Alfonso XI, is later incorporated into the kingdom of Granada.

In this epoch Ronda and its Serrania gain great importance in the history of the reconquest as she is coveted by everybody due to her situation on the frontier between the kingdoms conquered by the Christians and the Nazarite kingdom of Granada, and by changing allies and enemies with extraoedinary frequency, the fighting taking place from the XIII century on, either from Granada or from Christian lower Andalucia when the straits of Gibraltar became a problem of survival.

In 1359 Mohamid V of Granada was deposed by his brother Ismael, and he in turn by Abul Said Alhamar, «El Bermejo». Muhamed flees and seeks asylum in Fez and the Benemerines hand Ronda over to him. Restored to the Granada throne with the help of the Christians our town is incorperated into the kingdom of the Nazeries.

During the 15th. century Ronda comes down in the world due to the furious attacks from the christians.

In 1407 after the conquest of the village of Zahara, the infante Fernando sent his chief commander D. Ruiz Lopez Davilos with 2000 lancers in the hope of conquering Ronda.

But it was too strongly and well guarded with many defenders and winter was coming on.

The conquest of the city was not possible until the accession of the catholic kings to the throne of Aragon and Castile. They determine to finish once and for all with the Arab domination in Spain. Fernando the Catholic meticulously prepared the conquest of the Algarbe of Malaga to the west of the province. He succeeded totally in the campaign of 1485. With the conquest of Ronda on the 22nd. of May of the same year.

On the 15th. of April 1485 the king leaves Cordoba and marches towards Puente Genil and on the 19th. he has already positioned himself in Cartama, Coin and Benamaques.

Hamet el Zegri, governor of Ronda and head of the tribe of the same name leaves the city of Ronda in order to defend the villages besieged by Fernando the catholic.

Despite their courage and efforts Coin falls on April 27th. on the following day the same happens to Cartama.

After conquering the whole of the valley of Cartama the christian troops reach the gates of the city of Malaga, to where Hamet el Zegri manages to arrive with reenforcements and eventually save it.

On the 5th. of May the marques of Cadiz marches to conquer the city of Ronda accompanied by D. Pedro Enrique with 3000 horses and 8000 foot soldiers.

King Ferdinand marches towards Antequera and Archidona besieging the city of Loja in order to keep his troops from Malaga busy. At the same tpme he sends his artillery from Cartama and Coin and to Teba where the whole army has to meet in order to conquer the city of Ronda and where the marques of Cadiz had arrived first.

All these stratagems were necessary in order to conquer the impregnable city of Ronda.

On the 11th. of May the governor of Ronda, Hamet el Zegri heard that the true intention of the christian armies was not the conquest of Ronda but, by pretenting to besiege Ronda and Loja in order to distract his troops a second christian army would march to the final conquest of the city of Malaga which would logically be badly guarded.

The 12th. of May having arrived and Hamet el Zegri seeing the christian army camped round Ronda, did not doubt the news he had received. he prepared his army to march to the defense of Malaga, naming Abraham al haqui, as governor in his absence.

The siege of the city of Ronda was ordered for the 13th. its total army consisted of 9000 horse and 20.000 soldiers leaving as rearguard 4000 horse and 5000 infantry soldiers more.

Hamet el Zegri's rage was immense when he realised on his way to Malaga that Ronda was blockaded. He decided to return with his whole army and tried to break through the ranks of the loyal christians time and again, but all his efforts were in vain.

The circle around the city tightened and on the 14th an attack was ordered.

One decisive factor which accelerated its fall, was the massive use of artillery which was distributed to three points.

The first pointing towards the octogonal tower of the castle: the second at the low walls round the gate of Almocabar and the third on the eastern side of the town from the heights of Tejares, which totally dominated the town. It is noteworthy that in the conquest of Ronda lombards were used as an artillery instrument of war.

After a heavy siege of seven days and without water, for the Marques of Cadiz had cut off the supply to the town, a breach was opened in the octogonal tower which later crashed to the ground.

Vista
Panorámica

Amanecer

Sunrise

Alba

L'aube

Sonnenaufgang

Puerta de
Felipe V　⇨

Gate of Phillip V

Porta di Filippo V

Arc de Felipe V

Tor Philipp V

⇦

Murallas y
Puerta de Almocábar

Fortress and
Almocábar Gate

Mura e
Porta di Almocábar

Murs et
Porte de Almocábar

Stadtmauern und
Almocábar Tor

Ciudad de las
Maravillas

City of
Wonders

Cittá delle
Meraviglie

Ville des
Merveilles

Stadt der
Wundern

Ciudad de los Encantos   Enchanting City   Città di Incànti

Casa del Rey Moro

Ville Enchanteresse   Stadt des Zaubers

udería

ewish
Quarter

Quartiere
braico

Quartier
if

idisichen
tadtviertel

Minarete
de
San Sebastián

Minaret of
San Sebastian

Minareto di
S. Sebastiano

Minaret
de San
Sebastian

Minarett
von
San Sebastian

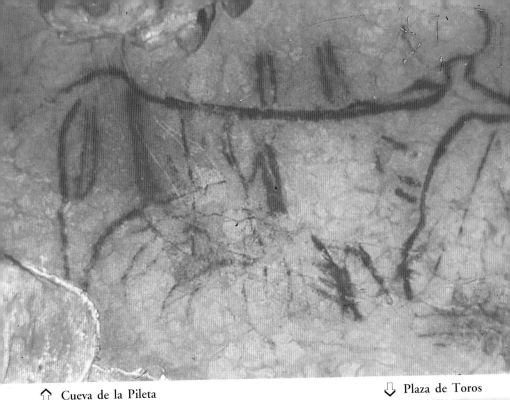

↑ Cueva de la Pileta   ⬇ Plaza de Toros

Foto Marcelino Pajares

So much and continuous was the artillery bombardment that the moors, who were protecting Cibda could scarcely hear each other, they had nowhere to sleep, nor did they know where to help because the bombardment was demolishing walls and houses.

In the middle of the battle, ensign Alonso Yañez Fajaro with his sword in one hand and the standard in the other and after many efforts managed to place the standard on the ruins of the tower. This gave great encouragement to the christian troops in their struggle and discouraged the moors who took refuge in the Alcazaba.

The governor, when he saw the desperate situation ran up the white flag, surrendering the city.

Hamet el Zegri after desperately trying to break the siege for ten days blinded by rage and courage returned with his men towards the city of Malaga in whose defense he died in 1487 not before cursing the defenders of the city of Ronda. Calling them traitors and weeping for the loss of his beloved city, The Flower of the kingdom of Granada.

King Fernando accepted a parley ordering the cessation of all hostilities and conceding their lives to the vanquished and only their furniture as property.

The christian captives crawled out of their dungeons and prisons half dead and extenuated. The majority of them had been taken prisoner in the battle of Axarquia, in number approximately 400. They were given food and clothing and sent to places of their own choice. In order to commemorate this event queen Isabel ordered their chains to be hung before the church of San Juan in Toledo.

The grater part of the moslem population went to the mountain villages under christian government. Others went to Africa and the most important personalities went to Alcala de Guadaira in the province of Sevilla, where they were given houses and properties.

The standards of the catholic church, the crusades and of the king of Castille were placed on the keep of the castle and on the 24th. of May king Fernando V of Aragon entered the city of Ronda in triumph.

The old mosque was converted and consecrated to the christian cult under the patronage of Santa Maria de la Encarnacion and to whom queen Isabel had a great devotion.

A solemn Te Deum was sung there and returning to the ruins of the octagonal tower king Fernando orderd a church under the patronage of the Holy Spirit to be built, for the conquest that year coincided with Whisuntide.

Wishing to join the queen who was waiting impatiently in Cordoba, he marched there entering in triumph, having left the count of Ribadeo, D. Pedro de Villandrado as governor of Ronda.

After the conquest of Ronda a distribution of lands to the nobles and knights who had participated in the conquest of the town was made. On the 25th. day of July 1485 in Cordoba, the town was given the faculty of governing itself by the same laws and jurisdiction which the towns of Sevilla and Toledo possessed, and the symbols on its royal houses consisted of a golden yoke with its parted straps and silver arrows on a red background.

Ronda was converted to the lordship of prince D. Juan, son of the catholic kings who married Margaret of Austria, and who on his death retained the overlordship of the city.

In 1499 the princess went to Flanders and then began the irregularities in the honourable administration of the city, taxes on food products, which came into the city were considerably augmented. Under these circumstances the purveyors decided to remain on the outskirts of the city and start small markets, which were the origins of quarters called 'el Mercadillo' and 'San Francisco'.

In time the 'San Francisco' quarter became the agricultural quarter and the "Mercadillo" continued to grow to its present size built on the north side of the Tajo.

Due to the morisco uprising in our Serrania and in the Sierra of Granada because they had not totally submitted to the capitulation agreed to at the conquest of Granada between king Boabdil and king D. Fernando, Ronda became the centre for expeditionary forces which attempted to subject the rebels; but after the reverse suffered by D. Alonso de Aguilar, the Gran Capitan's brother, at the hands of the moriscos and things being in a bad state, the catholic kings came to Ronda and stayed at a palace today known as Mondragon palace.

From then on the Serrania was sometimes at peace and at other times threatened by the Moriscos, until finally in 1609, by a royal decree, of Phillip III, the latter were finally expelled from Spain.

Important actions took place in our history. After the uprising of the Castilian «comunidades» the representatives of the most important Andalusian towns gathered in La Rambla, in the province of Cordoba and decided on their positions towards the "Comuneros". Ronda remained loyal to Charles I.

When the decisions of that meeting of the 17th. of February 1521 came into the hands of the king, who recognising the loyalty of our town towards him exclaimed personally "Oh Ronda, faithful and strong". This declaration has become the slogan on our coat of arms. Which had already been granted by the Catholic Kings and was ratified by the emperor himself in a letter dated the 26th. of September of that same year.

Life continued in Ronda. As she lacked a patron saint St. Christopher was chosen. The long street of commerce today called Armiñán became the principle street, asylums a hospital and in the Mercadillo, shops, inns and taverns were built.

The two centuries XVI and XVII shaped our beloved Ronda as we know it today. The principal part Madina which is now known as "La Ciudad", (The Town); the upper district which from now will be called "The Espiritu Santo" district, and the lower quarter, abandoned by its inhabitants and where they install their brothels, tanneries, and other industries, will be called San Miguel, and will be dedicated to The Holy Cross. The new quarter of the "Mercadillo" (the market), and San Francisco will be the symbols of new developement and of a new society.

Many years later, it is interesting to note, that Ronda heroically opposed the French invasion, for its mountain people do not allow themselves to be dominated very easily.

Nonetheless on the 10th. of February 1810 Joseph Bonaparte entered Ronda, lodging in the house of the marques of Moctezuma.

During the time the French remained in Ronda there were numerous acts of resistance by the people of Ronda who attempted to throw out the invadors. Finally they succeeded when a man from the mountains shot the French general Boussain on the outskirts of Ronda.

When the invadors left our city they destroyed the old Arab Alcazar (Fortress) and many other artistic monuments of great value.

Pedro Romero. Picture by Cuso

THE VISIT

And now that you know a little of our history we will begin our visit from here.

This is la Plaza de España. In it you can see the building with arches and arcades, that was the Town Hall, until 1980.It dates from 1843, but perhaps you would like to know that now the Town Hall is in the old military barracks on the old Town Square.

In the centre of the square there is a bust of D. Antonio Rios Rosas, a famous "Rondeño" who became a minister and president of the congress in 1862. He was distinguished by his honesty and eloquence. The other buildings, as you see, match the central building of the square.

Well, let's go along Rosario Street, on the right here. Here you can see some houses built in the style of the XVIIIth. century, with the classical grills and windows of Ronda.

We will now turn to the right along Los Remedios Street and enter Mina Street.

We will go into the gardens.

Come here, to the right, so that you can see the gorge in all its splendour, and the bridge from its foundation up.

This is the New Bridge, "The Bridge of Ronda". And I call it this,as the whole world calls it so, because really this symbolises the town in all its aspects.

Contemplate this masterpiece, spanning the gorge at its deepest, but also narrowest. This is really impressive, rousing pleasure and fear at the same time.

It was built by D. Juan Martin Aldehuela, an Arogonese architect from the village of Manzanera in the province of Teruel.

He began this work in the year 1751 on the foundations of another bridge.

He was helped by master builders from this town, among whom D. Antonio Diaz Machuca is worth mentioning, His machinery, invented by him for this task, was admired by all the engineers who came to see the construction.

– What do you mean machinery created by this master?

Well, this man who was a Rondeño invented several machines and apparatus with which, and with the help of 3 or 4 men, sufficient material could be lowered in a day which would employ 200 men for a week.

The work was finished in the year 1793, which means that it took 42 years to build. It is 98 metres high and is built entirely of blocks of stone.

It rises on its foundations from the depth of the gorge. it is formed at its base by a small arch, upon which is raised a central arch (which has a great room above it) and two smaller lateral arches.

There is a chamber under the centre of the bridge which was formerly used as a prison, the entrance is through a square building to the right which used to be the guard tower.

Look from here, you can see perfectly both from the left and the right of the bridge the remains of the foundations and columns of the former bridge.

It was built 1735 and consisted of only one arch. It stood for only five years.

– I have heard that the architect of this bridge committed suicide in order never to have to build another such in his life?

Look, this is a very romantic story and there are several variations, but the truth is that. D. Juan Martin Adelhuela died in Malaga, where his remains lie in a parish of that town.

Look, behind us there is a plaque which Ronda dedicates to its sister town Cuenca. Those houses built on the very edge of the precipice we call 'The Hanging Houses of the Tajo'.

Ronda has, due to its situation, a great similarity to the city of Cuenca.

– And what is that old building opposite us?

That is the Convent of Santo Domingo, the Catholic kings ordered it to be built. When it was finished it was handed over to the patronage of the Dominican friars. Of the original building only the church is left but

A woman was the cause of my downfall

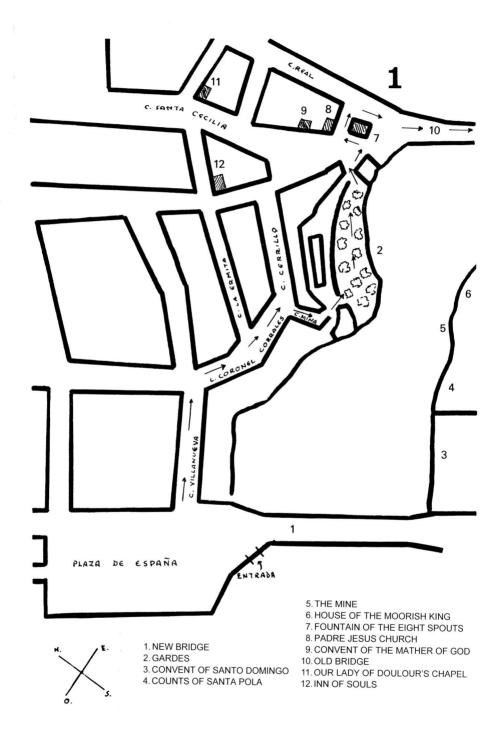

1

C. REAL

11

C. SANTA CECILIA

9 8 7

10

12

C. LA ERMITA

C. CERRILLO

C. MINA

CORRALES

L. CORONEL

C. VILLANUEVA

2

6

5

4

3

1

PLAZA DE ESPAÑA

ENTRADA

N.
E.
O.
S.

1. NEW BRIDGE
2. GARDES
3. CONVENT OF SANTO DOMINGO
4. COUNTS OF SANTA POLA

5. THE MINE
6. HOUSE OF THE MOORISH KING
7. FOUNTAIN OF THE EIGHT SPOUTS
8. PADRE JESUS CHURCH
9. CONVENT OF THE MATHER OF GOD
10. OLD BRIDGE
11. OUR LADY OF DOULOUR'S CHAPEL
12. INN OF SOULS

no worship is celebrated there now. Its entrance is on the so called slope of Santo Domingo at the end of the brigde on the left. It has three naves, and an elavated half orange shape, with a beautiful panelled cieling, in the Mudejar style with a choir. The building after having been abandoned by the friars during the dissolution, it then became Ronda's first covered market, 1850, later it was used for other activities.

The inquisition was held in this convent.

We must also mention that in this church there is a mausoleum with the remains of D. Jose de Moctezuma y Rojas and those of his wife.

He had it built in his life time and at his expense and it occupies the site of the former chapel del Rosario.

– What beautiful houses can be seen from here?

You are right, it is the north eastern part of the city, and from these terraces the over all view is marvellous.

These terraces are of recent construction, they were built by the Town Hall, bent on beautifying and bettering the city. From them the contemplation and stonework of the Tajo and the city has been enhanced, and also the peerless view of the bridge and the remains of the convent of Santo Domingo and the house of Los Guerreros Escalantes, known as the House of the Counts of Santa Pola.

– Which one? The one with the Arab windows and arches?

As you can see it is a manor house with many Arab remains. It was built on the remains of an Arab shrine, as a matter of fact it was the tomb of an Arab noted for his life and for his virtues, what we would call a good man.

On the portal we can see a large heraldic coat of arms of the Guerreros de Escalantes.

But let us continue down. Look from this corner at the view of the Old Bridge and of the gorge.

This bridge has been at times called Arabic and even Roman, but this must be clarified, it was reconstructed in the year 1616, on the foundations of an original Arabic one.

It consists of only one arch, 10 metres in diameter and 31 metres above the level of the river and it is 30 metres long and 5 metres wide.

Until the end of the last century there was an inscription on it which. D. Jose Moreti has transmitted to us and which I am going to reproduce. It goes thus:

Ronda rebuilt this construction under its joint corregidor with Marbella, D. Juan Antonio Torubio de Quñones for the king our lord in the year 1616.

What do you think of the view that we enjoy from here?
– Beautiful, but tell me, what is that aristocratic ochre coloured house?
It is called the House of the Moorish King.
– Ah! that is the house with the remains of the entrance of the sultanas baths, built by the Arabs.
Listen, now we are going to abandon flowery speeches, romanticism and legends and we will go to the truth.
This building was not constructed for a sultana's baths, nor for any thing like that, for the only thing that this does is to increase our fantasy and lead us away from the truth.
The Mine or shaft constructed by Abomelic around the beginning of the XIV century as a military edifice. Ronda in the XIV century, being the capital of the kingdom of the Benimerines in this part of Spain which also included Gibraltar, was the most important natural fortress in the whole of the southern part of the peninsula.
The stairs were built in the live rock, partly protected by brichks and adobe, with a few hollows and windows in order to let in the light, and a few rooms or extensions used as dungeons where the prisoners slept. The whole staircase is vaulted and built in sections, One can deduce from this visit that it really was of military origin.
In times of sieges, fights and civil wars the Arabs used to form a human chain of christian slaves, drawing up water from the depth of the river into the interior of the town. The said stairway is well camouflaged and on its inside walls can be seen the marks and signs made by the slaves who worked there.
There is a proverb about the stairway that says:
In Ronda you will die heaving up water skins.

42

During the reconquest of Ronda it was discovered by the Marquis of Cadiz and it was guarded so that no-one should escape that way.

– But tell me: during droughts or blockades of the river it was impossible to get water out of it. What was the use of this shaft?

Look, opposite the access door there is a fountain which still supplies Ronda today and formerly the water ran down the river towards the entrance door to the shaft in the depth of the Tajo. Well, this stairway is at the back door of the so called 'House of the Moorish King' axactly opposite the spring.

This 'House of the Moorish King' is a misnomer. The historian Hernan del Pulgar tells us about the shaft when he describes the conquest of Ronda and our compatriot vicente Espinel in his Life of Marcos de Obregon's squire refers to it as one of the most important remains from Arab domination in Spain. But the house, except possibly a few Arab vestiges in its gardens, dates from the beginning of the XVIII century and was restored at the beginning of the last century.

Its facade has some tiles representing a moorish king, perhaps Abomelic, in a hieratic position. Its balconies are Ronda forged, with some Sevillan tiles, all from the beginning of this century as I have said.

Now this house is as well known in the world as is the Tajo or the bridge. People from all over the world are interested in it and this fame is due to Dá Trinidad Schultz, Duchess of Parcent.

This lady of great beauty and intelligence bought the house from Mr. Perrin of Baltimore, U.S.A. at the beginning of the XXth. century.

She enriched it with the best furniture, paintings, ceramics and decorations which she brought from all over the world. She had the most important families of that epoch visit it and gave Ronda fame both on account of her house and because she encouraged local arts to surge up again.

But a certain section of Ronda did not agree with her ideas and she suffered some persecution. The last straw was a coffin with her initials on, which appeared on the square named after her, in the garden laid out with her money. This action made her decide to sell the house. To Alexander Machinley, the American President's grandson and she left Ronda with a heavy heart.

This lady, whose family originated rom Malaga married D. manuel de Iturbe, called viceroy of Mexico, because of his immense fortune. Their daughter Dña. Piedad Iturbe married Prince Hohenlohe, kaiser William II cousin, they are the parents of D. Alfonso Hohenlohe.

Later the duchess married the duke of Parcent and after his death became the dowager duchess of Parcent.

But let us continue, time does not pass in vain. We are now in Mine Street whose paving is a reproduction of the old Ronda style.

What a beautiful square.

This is where the Mercadillo begins.

– The Mercadillo?

Yes Sir, for us this is the modern town, built on the north side of the Tajo, the Mercadillo.

– And why?

Listen, its beginnings are really very interesting and I am going to tell you about them, so that you can see that in this town even the names and simple things are history.

When Dña. Margaret of Austria, widow of D. Juan left Ronda to return to Flanders in 1499, the administration and government of Ronda suffered great changes. The excises and taxes which were demanded at the gates of Ronda dissuaded the sellers from bringing in all sorts of articles. These latter instead of bringing their products to the usual places, left them on the plain at the doors of the town, at the principal gate Almocabar or in the Ejido zone, the gate at the bridge.

The repeated attempts of the authorities to stop these abuses proved useless, in fact, they were the origin of commerce and the fairs which have been so important to Ronda.

To the south of the city, opposite the principal gate, that of Almocabar, on the flat ground by the entrance, there was a hermitage to the Visitation. Around it there were about a hundred stalls or little shops where the traders began to lodge in order to save on the taxes for entrance into the city.

Because of their wish to emulate, the traders situated at the Ejido by the bridge, in other words, where we now are, also erected a chapel, today called Padre Jesus. This image and that of our Lady of Doluours attract great devotion in the town of Ronda.

The facade is gothic, even though one can see renaissance influences in the bell tower, having been reformed several times, the last, the actual building in 1755.

The church is not very large but it is well distributed, divided into three naves separated by two brick columns, and two other columns on either side with capitels bordered with flowers in relief. These colunms support the central nave which has a beautiful coffered cieling.

Notable people of Ronda were baptised in this church, such as Vicente Espinel a man of letters, and Rios Rosas a politician or the bullfighter Cayetano Ordóñez "Niño de la Palma".

The square and the Calle Real (Royal Street) was until the middle of the last century the commercial centre of Ronda. The Fountain of Eight Spouts, which was the public fountain for the inhabitants of that district. It is a simple fountain with eight spouts, from which it derives its name, with a big trough at the back to water the animals.

It is not known when it was built, but traces in its structure shows it to have been built or restored in the time of Charles III. It is the most typical fountain with dash in Ronda; it has the town coat of arms with the yoke and arrows.

Near the church of Padre Jesus is the Convent of The Mother Of God, Which is one of the most beautiful corners of Ronda.

It is built in the Mudejar Gothic style recently restored.

In this convent which dates from the middle of the XVI century there has been preserved its church with a baroque altar in gilt and its principal courtyard.

Ascending to the first floor one can see a bautiful arch in mosaics and brick work which leads into the library.

From here, if you do not mind, we will return to the Old Bridge from where we will continue our visit, and allow me to show you the third bridge.

That bridge which you see down there at the entrance to the gorge, is the smallest and is another Arab Bridge, even though everybody calls it the Roman Bridge.

It was built during the Arab domination in the century XIV, it has been damaged by the rise and fall of the Guadalvin river and has had to be totally restored.

It is small and seems unimportant, but i would like you to know that it was the principal entrance into Ronda trough the old quarter, near the

Xijara gate, restored back in 1970 and the remains of which you can see over there in the walls.

– What are those ruins in the background, behind the bridge?

Those are the Arab Baths.

The building was the property of the duchess of Parcent, afterwards sold to Sr. Zini Vito, one of the pioneers for tourism in Ronda. It was he, who discovered, perhaps by chance, the remains of the baths which we are now going to see.

These were discovered, as I said, by Sr. Zini Vito, when a farm which was built on top of them, collapsed, when they were inmediately rediscovered because they were completely covered by sand, stones and other objects due to the swelling of the river.

When the 'Direccion de Bellas Artes' (Conservation Ministry) saw the importance of the said buildings they indemnified the said gentleman for all his work and efforts and took over the work themselves.

These baths are among the better preserved and interesting in the whole of Spain, even though they have lost their marbles, gypsium and mosaics with which the Arabs used to cover their buildings.

They were built approximately at the end of the XIII and beginning of the XIV centuries.

The baths consist of three rooms whose structures show what they were used for.

In the first hot room can be seen, very well restored by the Direccion General de Bellas Artes, the chimney for the outlet of smoke and hot air and the remains of a stove to heat the water that came from the well along channels. In this room can still be seen the channels along which the hot air passed to the central chamber.

This second central chamber is divided into thee naves covered with vaulting sustained on brick horseshoe arches. A few of these arches and their capitals have been restored; but there are some other very interesting ones, for example, a Roman capital very eroded by time, of great value which together with the lateral domes oblige one to stop and contemplate this chamber carefully.

From this cold room we will pass to the third which was the cold room in which everybody relaxed and was massaged.

When the andaluz weep, they sing.
The Author

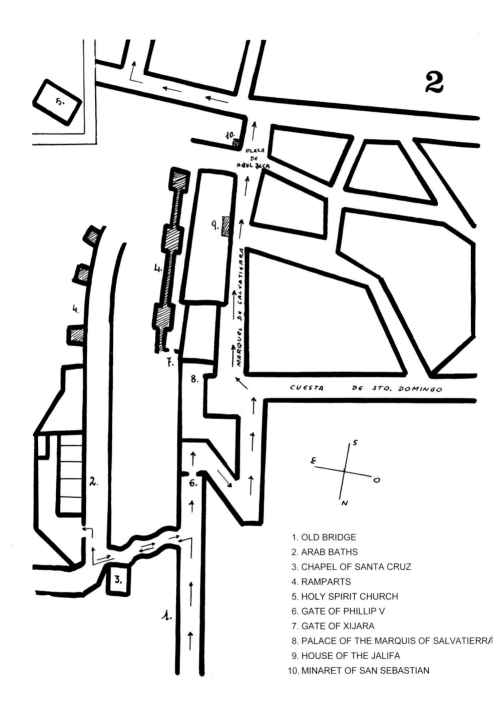

2

PLAZA DE ABUL BECA

MARQUEL DE CALVATIERRA

CUESTA DE STO. DOMINGO

1. OLD BRIDGE
2. ARAB BATHS
3. CHAPEL OF SANTA CRUZ
4. RAMPARTS
5. HOLY SPIRIT CHURCH
6. GATE OF PHILLIP V
7. GATE OF XIJARA
8. PALACE OF THE MARQUIS OF SALVATIERRA
9. HOUSE OF THE JALIFA
10. MINARET OF SAN SEBASTIAN

⬆ Convento de Sta. Isabel de los Angeles ⬇ Santa María La Mayor

Casita de la Torre - Sta. María

Mir hab

María Reina
de la Familia

← Virgen de los Dolores. Sta. María

Fachadas Casas Rondeñas   Tipical Façades   Façades Tipiques
Case Rondeñe   Typische Häuser

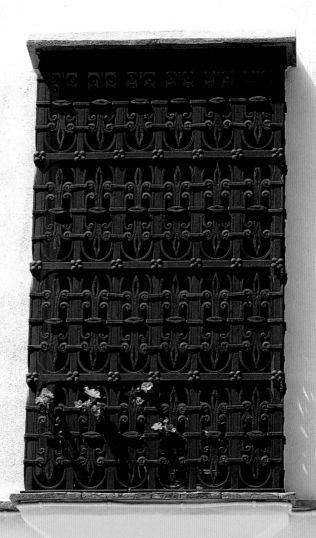

Rejas y Sombras   Grills and Shadows   Inferriate ed Ombre   Ombres et Grilles

engittern und Schatten

Passing through a door we come into a water deposit or fountain without its original covering of bricks. It is very well preserved and could have been used as a place for ablutions before entering the principal building.

These baths were surrounded by various buildings and industries, the archaeological value augments day by day, as work on the excavation continues.

Do you like it? Look up and see our restored walls and the gate of Xijara:

It is the gate about which I spoke before, but you can see it better from the well, it is that higher building, on the corner.

Arab towns were fortified as is this town. Ronda was fortified with three walls or ramparts whose remains you can see perfectly from down here and which gives one a great feeling of strengh.

The first of these ramparts starts from those towers that you see continuing from the baths; from the second start the pincipal ones, and above them the fortified houses were like a third rampart. Between the remains of the first and second ramparts was the old quarter and the Jewish quarter. This quarter gradually disappeared after the conquest of Ronda by the Catholic Kings because the jews and mudejares who lodged there were in the habit of helping their coreligionists who had taken refuge in the mountains, making it very easy for them to penetrate the town by night in order to plunder and obtain provisions.

– What is that building that looks like a chapel or a hermitage?

That is the chapel of Santa Cruz. In this hermitage, the owners, masters and workers in the leather factories, potteries and other trades which have desappeared, worshipped. It has been restored by the Direccion General de Arquitectura.

Well now let's go up the hill and rest at the gate of Philip V.

Here on the right you have a plaque saying that this gate was built during the reign of Phillip V. in the year 1742.

It has been proved that when the old bridge was built in the year 1616 there was a gate called Bridge gate until in the year 1742, on receiving its present structure the name was changed to that of Phillip V.

Let us continue up and enjoy this ascent for its pleasantness and the beauty of its streets and houses.

Detalles de Ronda

Here we have the Palace of the marquis of Salvatierra.

It was built at the end of the XVIIIth. century and the actual structure dates from that time. it was built on the site of some Arab houses, and it belongs to the marquises of Salvatierra and de Parada who live in it at varioua time of the year.

The building is of great artistic and historic value in the interior, but it is a private residence. It has a magnificent façade in the barroque style with double corinthian columns on each side with some suns on its doorhead. Above this there is a beautiful Ronda forged balcony, it is made with forged and sculptured iron.

On the upper part of the façade can be seen the figures of four peruvian Inca Indians which reveal a colonial influence. Their postures are very simple, for the first is a young girl who is timidly trying to hide her nakedness, and the second is a naughty boy who is putting his tongue out in a gesture of mockery. The figures on the other side represent the same characteristics.

Above all this in the centre is the family coat of arms.

If you like we will continue up the Salvatierra Street.

– Yes, whatever you say.

Look at these interesting and picturesque streets.

– Are the majority of these houses being restored?

Yes, but all under the direction of the General de Arquitectura, so that they neither break up nor lose the atmosphere of this quarter.

Look at this house to the left, with its two coats of arms.

It is the House of the Jalifa.

Of the Jalfaifa?

Yes, if was here that the last Jalifa of Tetuan, when morrocco was a Spanish protectorate educated his children and maintained his family.

Well the hill is finished and we will rest for a few minutes in this square called Abul-Beca, in memory of a famous Arab poet born in Ronda in the XIIIth. century.

Here we have the Minaret of San Sebastian so called because the mosque that occupied the site until the conquest of Ronda was converted into a church under the patronage of San Sebastian.

Of the said mosque and church only the tower of the minaret remains. Built in the XIVth. century by the Nazarites it has been restored, notice a few ornamental remains and mudejar constructions.

In the lower part you can notice a beautiful horse shoe arch and the interlacing bricks, and a few ceramic remains that originally decorated the whole tower.

We continue along Armiñan St., turn left and then right and arrive at the PLAZA DE LA CIUDAD (the town square). In the centre of the square is the monument to the Duchess of Parcent (1866-1937). This used to be the parade ground of Ronda. It is one of the most typical squares of the town. Until 2001, in the centre of the square, there was a bust of the distinguished writer of Ronda, Vicente Espinel (1550-1624). His statue is now in the Plaza del Gigante, 2004. He was a friend of Lope de Vega and of Miguel de Cervantes, frequently having long chats with the latter when he was in Ronda and when D. Miguel de Cervantes lodged in the Posada de las Animas (The Inn of Souls), today it is an old age pensioner's home. Vicente de Espinel's musical side is unknown to many people; but he was a good musician who added the fifth string to the Spanish guitar.

On this square from left to right we have first the Church of Charity from the XVIth. century. founded by the Rondeño Pedro de Miranda in order to serve as a place of burial for condemned and unknown persons, Today it is occupied by the sisters of the Cross.

Round the corner from this building there existed a poor house for poor passers through, to lodge in.

More to the left, is the church and convent of Santa Isabel de los Angeles, the Clare nuns, it was built in the middle of the XVIth. century.

Opposite the cathedral, on the other side of the gardens, stood the Castle of laurel under Roman domination, converted into an Arab fortress.

On the 26th. of August 1812, it was dynamited by the French when they left Ronda, thinking that they would return they calculated that in this way they would encounter no resistance once all the missiles, powder and bombs stored there to be used by the Spaniards in their defence, had been destroyed.

As you will remember Ronda as a natural fortress was very well protected by the hand of God who defended it with ravines and gorges; but it had, and has a natural access just behind the ruins of the castle of Laurel. This is where its principal door was to he found, the gate of Almocabar. A second gave access to the Alcazaba, was the gate of Images which also disappeared in the said explosion.

3

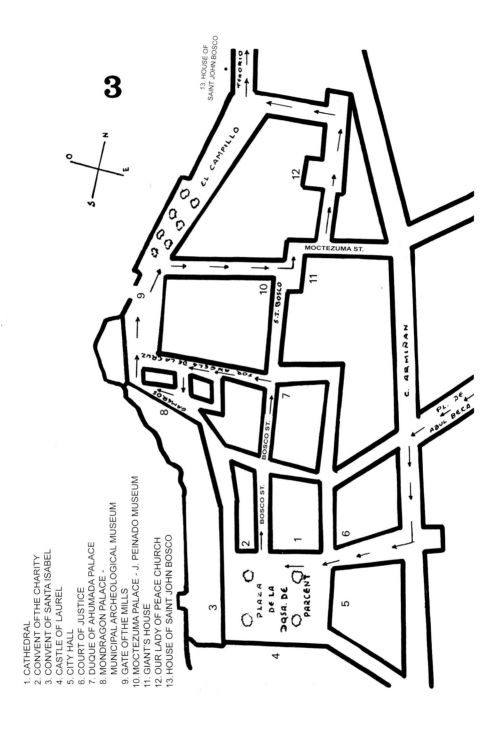

1. CATHEDRAL
2. CONVENT OF THE CHARITY
3. CONVENT OF SANTA ISABEL
4. CASTLE OF LAUREL
5. CITY HALL
6. COURT OF JUSTICE
7. DUQUE OF AHUMADA PALACE
8. MONDRAGON PALACE -
MUNICIPAL ARCHEOLOGICAL MUSEUM
9. GATE OF THE MILLS
10. MOCTEZUMA PALACE - J. PEINADO MUSEUM
11. GIANT'S HOUSE
12. OUR LADY OF PEACE CHURCH
13. HOUSE OF SAINT JOHN BOSCO

13. HOUSE OF
SAINT JOHN BOSCO

EL CAMPILLO

TENORIO

MOCTEZUMA ST.

S.T. BOSCO

SOR ANGELA DE LA CRUZ

CARMONA

BOSCO ST.

BOSCO ST.

C. ARMIÑAN

PL. DE
ABUL BECA

PLAZA
DE LA
SQSA. DE
PARCENT

Orson Welles. Picture by Cuso. 1964

From the southern part of the city can be seen, and even better from the slope of the Images, the remains of the ramparts and towers, which are today called the Castle.

It was Salesians school until 2004, the foundation Moctezuma, because the marquis of Moctezuma promised and brought to Ronda Augustins and Salesians. inicially the Salesians occupied the manor house of the marquis, today Joaquin Peinado Museum. When the Augustins left they took over the direction of the Castle.

Continuing with the buildings in the square we find the Old Military Barracks.

This building was constructed in 1651, as you can read on the inscription discoverd on the façade; it was restored in 1734 ad again in 1818. It was at this time when its original entrance was changed and the building suffered a great transformation.

The back of this building which gives into the Armiñan Street, has one of the oldest stores which are conserved in Ronda. It was the old public granery and in the lower parts were the old silos for the grain.

It is being restored by the Direccion General de Arquitectura for the Town Hall, 1980. Every attempt is being made to preserve the original beauty of the building, adding others, such as a coffered Mudejar cieling of the XVIth. century, donated by the countess of Santa Pola, a direct hieress of the Guerreros de Escalantes, no better place could have been chosen for its preservation than the dome in the entrance to the City Hall.

– Tell me, on its façade is the coat of arms of Ronda but the one on the left, from where is it?

The one on the left is from the town of Cuenca, sister town of Ronda, an agreement come to in the year 1975.

The white building with the coat of arms of the catholic kings on its façade is today the Court of justice, it was the first Town Hall following the standards set by the Catholic Kings for the good governmwnt of their kingdoms and landowners, But according to legend and contrary to histo-rical evidence, Dña. Margarita of Austria, sovereign Lady of this principality and wife of Don Juan, son of the catholic kings and heir to the throne. he did not live to occupy it as he died when he was a student at Salamanca.

This building has had different uses since Dña. Margeret left for her native Flanders, ending up as a court of justice today.

– Listen, regarding this, I would like to explain something to you that perhaps you do not know. So you can rest a little, because truly you have not stopped talking.

– Do you know since when the colour black has been a sign of mourning and sorrow for the loss of a dear one in families in Spain?

Well no, I don't know really.

– The catholic kings felt such sadness and sorrow at the loss of their son D. Juan that they changed the national tradition of white for mourning into black.

Very interesting, thank you.

Well, now we have in front of us one of the most important monuments of the city.

Santa Maria la Mayor is beautiful both inside and outside, it is interesting and mysterious at the same time.

The façade itself tells us about the building, of its history and its beauty. Different from the façades of churches and cathedrals to which we are accustomed, the tower, which you can see from every part of the city, tells us of its charecteristics and design, of all the alterations and constructions which this building has suffered in its time. A mudejar tower built on the foundations of a minaret it is topped with a beautiful renaissance belfry.

On the right side there is a lovely long balcony built in the reign of Phillip II, 1582, they were to be the boxes, from which the nobles and authorities of the city of Ronda could watch the jousts, bullfights and other public acts.

Entering through the little tower door, to the right, we pass through a room where the remains of the mirhab arch of the mosque can be found, adorned with inscriptions and arabesques from the nazarite dynasty and which reminds us of the oratory of the Alhambra at Granada.

This mosque was built at the end of the XIIIth. century and the beginning of the XIVth.

Let us go in and we shall see that the building is bigger than we had expected from the outside.

Built in the highest part of the city, we are told that in this very same place there had been a temple erected to the memory of Julius Ceasar, of which nothing remains except perhaps, some possible remains of the foundations and a plaque which until recently historians referred to, and on which one can read IVLIO DIVO MUNIPES to commemorate the victory of Julius Ceasar over Pompey's sons, Cneus and Sextus at the battle of Munda in the year 45 B.C.

Those same walls would be used for the later construction of the pincipal mosque and then later still for the pincipal church of Ronda.

The mosque was converted into a church devoted to Sta. maria de la Encarnación, to whom Isabel was very devoted.

King Ferdinand granted it the category of Abbey. It had honours and devotions which are stipulated for cathedrals and its chapter was allowed to nominate parish priests for Ronda, Arriate, Cuevas del Becerro and Serrato until the concordat of 1851 in which the size of the greater parish was reduced.

The building itself is in two very different architectural styles.

The part to the south is late gothic from the end of the XVth. century with on its right side renaissance influence because of the restoration it had undergone after an earthquake befell this city in 1580 and which damaged its most important buildings.

Here we have the beautiful baroque high altar from the end of the XVIIIth. century, with numerous vegetable decorative motifs, salmonic columns, fretwork etc:, gilt and polychromed on its lower parts. It has the images of the Immaculate Conception and St. Ann with the infant Virgin. On the left there is a churrigueresque altar also from the end of the XVIIIth. century, a reliquary altar has an Our Lady of Doulours of La Roldana.

To the right of the high altar gtere is a fresco of St. Cristopher painted by a painter from Ronda called Jose de Ramos in 1798, which reminds us of the great paintings of this saint in the Spanish cathedrals of Seville, Toledo etc:.

In the centre is the choir, which cuts it in two.

The choir is by unknown builders. It was finished in 1736 in the baroque style, the lower choir stalls are of walnut wich litanies motifs and the rest in cedar wood with very good carvings of saints and apostles.

Only one of the organ cases, built in 1710 in this church remain.

In the centre there is a walnut lectern by local carvers, with 4 books of gregorian chant that still exist in the church today.

These are XVIIth. century choir books, of parchment illuminated and in polychrome of great artistic merit value.

On the wall behind the choir, the Vialucis of the Virgin Mary (1997-2000) by the sculptor Francisco Parra, born in Seville in 1961. It is a work of art consisting of 14 stations in bronze presided by the image of Mary, Queen of the Family.

After the earthquake of 1580, in which the northern and western part of the church was destroyed, it was decided to enlarge it.

A church was built, a replica of Granada Cathedral in renaissance style, with corinthian and tuscan columns. This contruction took until 1704.

This part of the church consists of three naves. In the centre there is a great dome with 4 medallions which represent the 4 evangelists. It is sustained by 4 great columns, two in corinthian style with large cornices and the other two in Tuscan style. There are 4 large entrance doors. The high altar was built in 1727 by Esteban de Salas the presbitery. The next year the pulpit in carrara marble was built.

I have to explain that the high altar of Esteban de Salas was destroyed in 1936. To fill this noticibly empty space in the church the lateral altar of the Sacred Heart of Jesus has taken its place today.

This altar, which was formerly a secondary one, is carved in red pine and attracts every visitor's attention for its magnificence, XVIIIth. century.

Worthy of mention are: the Sanctuary, jewel of the XVIIIth. century by Vergara the silversmith from Malaga and the front panel of the altar in white metal by Gonzalo Angulo from Lucena, but most of all the titular statue of the church, Our Lady of the Incarnation, by the sculptor from Seville, Manuel Ramos Corona, in 2003.

To the right of this altar is the sacristy with the remains of the church treasure, another eighth gregorian chant choir books, XVIIth. and XVIIIth. century chasubles, a marble changing table for the priests and a few documents referring to church matters.

If we take the street immediately to the right ox the cathedral we come into the Moctezuma street. We shall come across many manorial houses in this part of the city, with their heraldic coats of arms which tell us about the history of these families.

For example, this one to the right is the house of the dukes of Alhumado, founder of the Civil Guard, or this other one to the left which belongs to the Hinojoso Bohorquez family, a house with one of the most beautiful patios in the city of Ronda.

We will continue along the Sor Angela de la Cruz street and we will come to the Mondragon Palace, today Archeological Museum.

Among all these white houses there is one aristocratic one in stone, which is why it is commonly called the "Stone House". It is clearly an exponent of the cultures, styles and civilizations through which Ronda's civil architecture speaks to us.

This building which was originally built by Abomelic, king of Ronda at the beginning of the XIVth. century (1314) has been the seat of kings and governors. From there Hamet el Zegri governed this province under the Nazarite domination.

Of that period there only remain the foundations and a few subterranean passages which run from the garden of the house to the old fortress of Ronda. In its walls one can see perfectly the changes and restorations that have taken place over the years. There are two mudejar style towers and an aristocratic renaissance style portal, with stone horse steps to assist horse mounting, a door into the stables and a mudejar style coffered ceiling in cedar wood which reminds us of the Spanish Golden century.

In its interior, in the old part there is what is called the arab patio, which in reality is mudejar and which clearly shows the restorations which have taken place in the palace.

Arab arches over renaissance decoration, restored old arab mosaics with mosaics of the XVIth. century.

It was over restored at the end of the XVIth. century by Melchor de Mondragon. Ascending to the first floor there is besides a large dome with family escutcheons, a large chamber with a mudejar coffered ceiling, the best in the palace.

The house was inhabited on two occasions by the catholic kings. The first time by D. Fernando in 1485 on the occasion of the conquest of Ronda and later by Isabel and Fernando in 1501 on account of the rebellion of the moriscos.

Later it passed into the hands of D. Fernando de Valenzuela, marquis of Villasierra a favourite of Mariana of Austria, widow of Phillip IV. D. Fernando de Valenzuela fell into disgrace and was deported to mexico dying there miserably.

We will leave Mondragon and go to the Plaza del Campillo, formely Puerta de los Molinos, and from its balconies we can see the old road that takes us to the city ramparts and its gate, today called the Gate of Christ. This was the access gate from the mills at the bottom of the Tajo into the town. From here we can see the gorge in its entirety and at its deepest with the handle of the cauldron at the very bottom and a beautiful view of the Mercadillo.

Let us return along Marquis of Moctezuma street and in the little square of San Juan Bosco we have on our right an old manor house with the coat of arms of the Moctezuma and Rojas family. This is the house built by d. Jose Moctezuma y Rojas, grandson in a direct line on the masculine side of the great emperor and king of Mexico, his tomb used to be in the church of Santo Domingo, and today his remains lie in the Palace Chapel itself, today Joaquin Peinado Museum.

Opposite is the Casa del Gigante (the Giant's House), the name was given to it by the people of the town because on its façade there is an effigy of a Punic Hercules found in the house and whose ciclopean shape gives it the aspect of a giant.

This house, which was built in the XIVth. century, is an example of a middle class arabic house.

In its interior it has a central patio with an old well surrounded by columns, and two chambers where one can see the remains of decorative moorish plaster work on their walls, arches and spandrels, which remind us again of the Alhambra of Granada, which was built during the nazarite period in Granada.

It has suffered different types of restoration because it has been put to different uses, such as for Mayor Ruiz Gutierrez de Escalante and later even as a home for abandoned children.

Let us continue down San Juan de letran street and we shall get to the square of the Beato Fray Diego Jose de Cadiz.

In this square is the house where the Beato Fray Diego Jose de Cadiz died, on the 24th. of may 1801, and the church of la Virgen de la Paz.

This church is devoted to the cult of the patron saint of Ronda, the oldest statues of the city of Ronda, to whom cult was rendered in the XVIth. century in the hermitage of San Juan de Letron, which has now disappeared.

The tradition of this statue goes back to the time of Alfonso XI but the actual statue seems more likely to be from the end of the XVIIth. century.

The temple possesses one nave only and several altars from the end of the XVIIIth. century.

It has a churrigueresque altar with an artistic shrine with mural paintings where the patron saint and mayoress of Ronda in perpetuity Our Lady of Peace stands.

At the feet of our Lady is a silver casket containing the remains of the Blessed Fray Diego.

In this church there is also a statue of Cristo de la Sangre which is venerated, it is by the famous statue maker from Sevilla Duke Cornejo, a pupil of Martinez Montañes, and a statue of Ecce-Homo of the school of Granada.

We will return to Armiñan street and back to the New Bridge, we shall cross the gorge and go over to the Plaza de España and on to the bullring. if you remenber, here we began the tour.

Here, my friend, we shall have to stop before going in, to explain to you not about the building but to let you know that you are entering the Ronda Bullring, the sanctuary of bull fighting on foot.

If our eyes as catholics look towards St. Peter's of Rome, and if the mohamedans look towards Mecca, the eyes of devotees of bull fighting look towards this place.

So, please look at its entrance, barroque, the exact opposite of the style of our schools of bullfighting which is classical and without any barroque, others may indulge in that.

It has tuscan columns supporting a broken pediment with the royal arms in the centre and a balcony of iron forged in Ronda with taurine motifs.

We shall enter so that you may see the bull fighter's cathedral of the world.

Before anything else I must say that our bullring belongs to the Real Maestranza de Caballeria (the Royal Institute of Knights) the chief 'Real Maestranza' of Spain, anterior to that of Sevilla, Granada, Valencia and Zaragoza.

It was founded by order of Phillip II in the year 1572, though its origins go back to the time of the catholic kings.

This institute was charged with the military education of the nobility, both as to horse riding and the use of arms, always having in view maintaining the activity of its members who in case of need should be ready to set out for any place in which they might be needed.

When the andaluz people become enraged they dance.
The Author

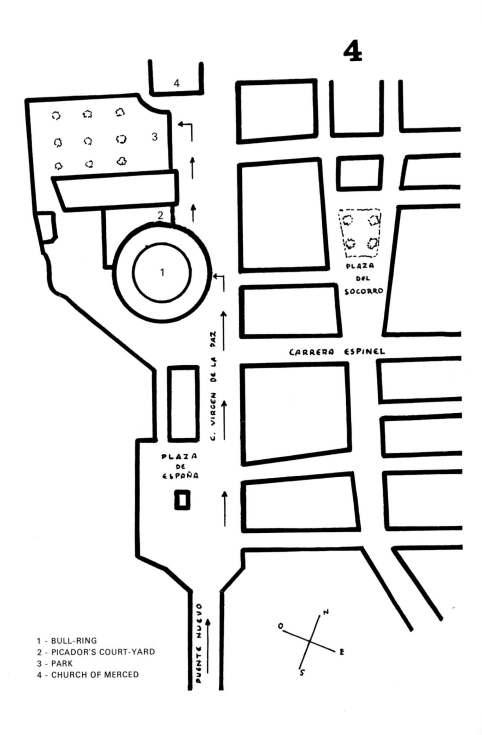

4

1 - BULL-RING
2 - PICADOR'S COURT-YARD
3 - PARK
4 - CHURCH OF MERCED

The deeds and battles of our 'Real Maestranza' since its foundation are innumerable.

But let us drop the 'Real Maestranza' who built this construction for their particular use rather than for bull fighting entertainments as we understand them today. well, as you know, before this building was erected the members used to have their bull entertainments and festivities on the parade ground, as I explained to you when we were visiting the old city.

The ring was inaugurated in may 1784. It is the widest ring in the world with a diameter of 66 metres and it is the only one that has a stone parapet. The exit for the bulls, the presidents' box and the royal box are situated on the same side of the ring, beside it is the only one that is totally covered.

It has 136 columns and nearly 5.000 seats.

The traditional "Goyesca" bullfight takes place there and lovers of bullfighting from all over the world come to learn what Ronda bullfighting is and to watch the art of bullfighting from our master Antonio Ordoñez.

This bull fight is enacted in memory of Pedro Romero, who according to the chroniches fixed and gave life to the golden rules of modern bullfighting.

Do you know that Pedro Romero was the master whom history relates killed 6.000 bulls.

– But, doesn't that seem a lot of bulls to you?

My friend, don't you know that besides killing 6.000 bulls he killed the 6.000 face to face.

He was born in Ronda in 1754 and entered on the life of bulls at eight years old. He left it at 72 and died at 90 without once having been wounded by the horn of a bull.

He was a director of the Sevilla school and founder of the Ronda one.

I told you that he entered on the life of a bullfighter at 8; I should have said that he was born a bullfighter.

Listen, and see if I am not right.

His grandfather D. Francisco Romero, began as is known, and as was the custom of his time: The bravest men used to stand in front of the bull, hat in hand, or a cape, but merely as a pastime. The bullfighting of that time, to call it something, was performed by knights on horse back, in other words spearing and wounding the valiant beast on horse back. He became so expert at it that he began to teach it, the use of the cape and how to kill under the rules he had acquired from his own experience and he invented the red cloth in order to kill the bull face to face placing before lovers of the sport the bull fighter's crew.

His father, Juan Romero was the one who organised the cuadrilla, (the bull fighter's crew) with picadors, banderilleros, etc.: and he died at 102 years old.

And, now you know all that he did! as if Pedro Romero had never heard bulls mentioned in his home!

On going out, the arch and gateway joined to the ring is the picadors entrance to the ring. It has the Spanish royal coat of arms the same as on the principal door.

This picador's courtyard was used as a yard for comedies before the Espinel theatre, now demolished, was built.

Now we will go to the Alameda or Park.

To the right we have the Iglesia de la Merced Carmelite convent founded by the Mercedarian order in the XVIth. century. Today it is occupied by H. H. Carmelites, who in their daily tasks produce typical local confectionary, for those who may require some, such as Ronda cakes or excellent home made bread.

Let us go into the Alameda which is the most important garden in Ronda.

It was laid out on the Ejido esplanade of the Mercadillo, in front of the convent de la Merced and finished in 1806.

Not one centime of municipal rates was spent on its outlay, for the work was paid for by the fines exacted from those who had either been obscene or provoked scandal on the streets.

The author of this ingenious and humourous idea was the then mayor of the town at that time, D. Vicente Cano.

The Alameda had several interesting things on the promenade by the Tajo, such as a series of busts of the whole royal family of Spain. At the entrance there were some inscriptions which I here reproduce for their curiosity and which no longer exist. They were removed during the Republic. D. Jose Moreti copied them and they go like this.

Palace of the marquis of Salvatierra

Calles y Plazas   Streets and Squares   Strade e Piazze   Rues et Places   Strassen und Plä

Plaza de Toros   Bullring   Arena

Les Arenes   Stierkampf Arena

Paco "El Herraó

da es Mujer Ronda is a Woman Ronda é una Donna Ronda est une Femme Ronda ist eine Frau

⬇ Patio de Santa Ana ⬆ Marqués de Salvatierra - Jardines Puerta Felipe V y Mercadillo

⇧ Palacio de San Juan Bosco ⇩

Virgen de la Paz Patrona de Ronda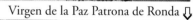

¡Oh Ronda mía! ¡Oh desgraciada!
¿Porqué incauto salí por tu Puerta de Almocábar?

Oh Ronda mia! Oh, Disgraziata!
Perché incauto uscii dalla tua Porta di Almocábar?

¡Oh ma Ronda! Oh malheureuse.
¿Pourquoi, moi, imprudent, t'ai je quittée par ta porte d'almocabar?

Oh my beloved Ronda! Oh unhappy one!
Why dit I thoughtlessly has through your gate Almocabar?

⇧ Palacio de los Hinojosas Bohórquez ⇨

Oh, mein Ronda, Du Unglückliche,
warun verliess ich Dich so unbedacht durch Dein Almocabar-Tor?

To the discreet town.

> *I have dedicated my enthusiasm to you*
> *And the money I have spent,*
> *So that this project may last*
> *Depends on your care.*
> *To the malicious Town.*
> *Oh! don't be surprised at my tears*
> *On seeing your lack of patriotism*
> *And your innate selfishness*
> *When you criticise this work.*
> *To the Ignorant Town.*
> *Of you foolish river,*
> *Who unable to criticise*
> *I only heard you murmur*
> *What a pity about the money!*
> *And another who said*
> *It's finished*
> *And it hurt no-one*
> *For no-one was asked for money*
> *For the cost*
> *Fell on those poor people*
> *Afflicted by their calamities*
> *And who were rescued at public expense.*

Now if you like we can go to the end of the park to look on the deepest part of the Tajo which on this side has a depth of 185 metres.

Do you know what this central balcony is called? It is the exclamation balcony, because everyone who comes here utters the most typical exclamation from his part of the world.

– What is the most typical one here in Ronda?

It is C...

That building that you see on the side of the hill is the Sanctuary de la Virgen de la Cabeza. It consists of a hermitage where the Virgen de la Cabeza is venerated and a country church. Where some hermits called the lonely ones lived during the XVIIIth. century.

The brotherhood of la Virgen de la Cabeza used to bring their virgin in a procession to Ronda during a very popular pilgrimage, which fortunately has not disappeared.

It is a very interesting place to go to because, apart from visiting the sanctuary there is a wonderful panoramic view of Ronda which is really fascinating.

Now that we are in the Alameda I want to show you a Pinsapo, for although we have seen several during our visit, because we generally have them in our squares, here there is a good example.

As I said before the Pinsapar is in the Sierra de las Nieves. In case on your return, you wish to see it, you turn off at km. 12 on the San Pedro road at the sign post Rajete, you go along it until you get to a farm called 'La Nava' and from there you can walk and see them. There you will find some very interesting examples and perhaps if you climb to the top of the Sierra de la Nieve to the summit of the Torrecilla which is at 1.919 metres, you may be able to see from Malaga to Gibraltar, that is to say the whole of the Costa del Sol and besides perhaps a cabra hispanica jumping about on the heights.

On your way out of Ronda I would like you to stop in the San Francisco quarter.

It will be very easy to recognise this sector because once you pass the ramparts all the white houses that you will see on your left and your right will be different from the rest of Ronda. You will now be in the San Francisco quarter.

I spoke of it before when I was explaining the origens of the Mercadillo.

It was born as a small market, when the traders at the end of the XVth. century refused to enter the city of Ronda in order to avoid paying the taxes and excises with which to swell the municipal coffers.

Some inns and taverns were built for traders and passers through and so a new quarter began which later would become the agricultural quarter, for the majority of traders decided to abandon the principal entrance to Ronda and to locate themselves to the north at the exit of bridge gate, today called Phillip V.

From the esplanade you can see the principal gate into Ronda. Puerta de Almocabar and the walls that separate the San Francisco quarter into two parts: the part that was built inside the ramparts and that on the outside, about whose beginnings I have spoken.

And sound of their guitar is their soul.
The Author

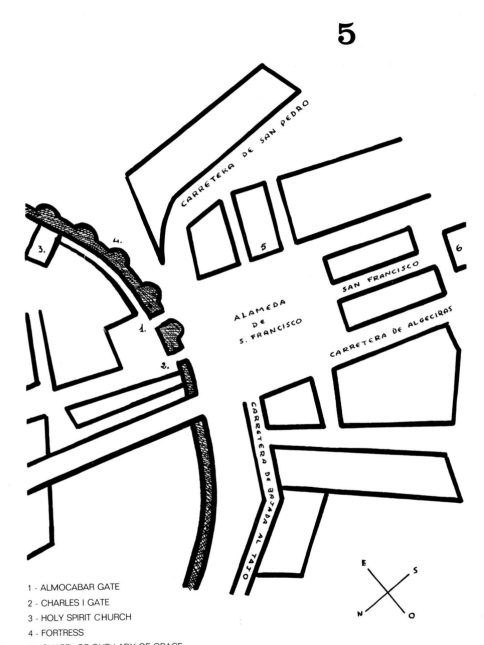

5

CARRETERA DE SAN PEDRO

ALAMEDA DE S. FRANCISCO

SAN FRANCISCO

CARRETERA DE ALGECIRAS

CARRETERA DE BAJADA AL TAJO

1 - ALMOCABAR GATE
2 - CHARLES I GATE
3 - HOLY SPIRIT CHURCH
4 - FORTRESS
5 - CHAPEL OF OUR LADY OF GRACE
6 - CONVENT OF SAN FRANCISCO

La Puerta de Almocábar (the cemetary gate) leads to the Alcazaba and to the city, though there was a second door, which has now disappeared the gate of the Statues of which we spoke when we were visiting the parade ground.

This gate bult in the XIIIth. century, consists of three doorways, with horse shoe arches between two semicircular towers which may have been sentry towers. On these towers there are some round stones in the form of crosses which were used during the conquest of Ronda in 1485. To the left there is another doorway, from the XVIth. century, built in the time of Charles I.

In the background you can see the remains of the Alcazaba, where the Salesian school now is and to the right is the Iglesia del Espiritu Santo (the church of the Holy Spirit).

This church was built on the orders of Fernando the catholic on the ruins of a Almohade octogonal tower which defended this natural access to the city and was destroyed by the christian lombards during the battle for the conquest of the city.

It was consecrated under the appellation of the Holy Spirit, because Ronda was conquered on the 20th. of May 1485, a day which in that year coincided with Whitsuntide.

It can easily be seen that it was built in time of war: it is sober and austere like a military fortress. It was finished in 1505 the year queen Isabel died.

It consists of one nave with a large pulpit, in keeping with that time in which the preacher could be easily seen and heard.

The nave is 30 metres long and 9 wide. it has great simplicity and the style is similar to Isabeline Gothic covered by later alterations. The barroque high altar occupies the central apse with a painting above of the coming of the Holy Spirit and in the centre, a painting on wood of 'La virgen de la Antigua' in a beautiful bizantine style.

On the high altar there are three coats of arms worked in stone, the central one has the imperial eagle of the house of Austria.

The belfry was built later as well as the door which was enlarged, and above which there is a niche with the Holy Spirit in the form of a dove.

On the present esplanade before the Puerta de Almocabar we can see the Capilla de Nuestra Señora de Gracia (Chapel of our lady of Grace). the patroness of the royal order of the knights.

It was the first temple on the new site in Ronda and it was built in the centre of the esplanade with the name Iglesia de la Visitacion. Later it was moved to the position it occupies today and named Virgen de Gracia.

As we are here it would be interesting to visit The Convent of San Francesco, on the outskirts of this quarter of the same name, it was founded by the catholic kings to commemorate the place monarch Fernando camped in during the siege of Ronda.

Damaged during the war of Independence, it still preserves a beautiful portal in the Isabeline style.

Under French domination a site was built which now lies in an educational and sports zone. It is to the morth of what is known as "The Fort".

The French governor of the town had it built, placing several canons and mortar pieces facing the town of Ronda in it and threatening to discharge them if the bands from the sierra did not stop harassing the French garrison in Ronda. Together with the mountaineers the citizens of Ronda used to attack the soldiers of the French garrison at night, making their lives impossible.

So innumerable are the beautiles of the city of Ronda as are innumerable the names of her illustrious citizens through the centuries who have carried with them the name of their beloved city through the whole world, some famous in the world of letters and others in arms.

To list their names would be interminable and you would not remember them, so if you will allow I will just refer to a few of them.

Don Vicente Espinel, an illustrious Ronda, writer, author of the picaresque novel "Vida del Escudero Marcos de Obregon", "The life of Squire Marcos Obregon", he was also an outstanding poet, creator of the Decima (a ten verse stanza), which is now called 'Espinela', he was one of the best musicians of Spain at the end of the XVIth. century.

He introduced the fifth string into the Spanish guitar, the so called prima, which gave the guitar a more popular character.

Don Antonio de los Rios y Rosas, an illustrious tribune and honoured politician.

He became a deputy, Minister and President of the congress in 1862, and ambassador to the Holy See. He declined other important positions and titles and those which he did fill he did so with dignity and honour, combating with great eloquence from the rostrum those whom he thought were not guiding the affairs of the government well.

D. Francisco Giner de los Rios (1839-1915), nephew of D. Antonio de los Rios y Rosas, can be considered as the master of liberal and lay intellectualism and he was the creator of the Institution of free Education.

Valle-Inclan, Azorin, Baroja, Antonio and Manuel Machado, Juan Ramon Jimenez, Ortega y Gasset, Perez de Ayala, Marañon, Azaña, Garcia Lorca, Dali, Buñuel, Guillen and others were influenced under his Institutions.

D. Fernando de los Rios (1879-1949), nephew and pupil of D. Francisco Giner de los Rios, was minister of Education, of Justice and minister of State during the Republic and embassador to the U.S.A. during the Civil war.

Joaquin Peinado (1898-1975), can be considered as the best painter born in this city.

He became a teacher in the College of Art in Malaga, later leaving for France where with his geniality in painting he became outstanding in the Parisian school of painting.

He was an intimate friend of Picasso.

– And what can you tell me about those Rondans that have triumphed in the art of bullfighting?

Listen, those gentlemen have not only triumphed: they have brought glory to the festival, founding a school in the difficult art of good bullfighting. Because, what do you think of the dynasty of the Romeros who gave life to bullfighting on foot? Or the dynasty of the Ordoñez, who have shown all over the world what real bullfighting is?

We will not continue as the discussion would become interminable. In letters, arts, politics and in folklore and in practically every cultural manifestation, Ronda counts on a great number of men whose fame is the logical complement which the greatness of man sets against the greatness of nature created by the fantastic situation of this city.

Besides that, my friend, I must tell you that I have not shown you all that there is to see in my beloved town. In order to do that we should need much more time and you say you have no more time.

But you must return and complete this visit the same as if it were an incomplete dream.

I could enumerate so many memories, odd corners and places that we have not been able to see or still have to see, that the list would be interminable; but when you do return you will have to visit the little temple of Our Lady of Dolours.

Built in the time of Ferdinand VI about the year 1734, It is situated in the place where the condemned to death were executed and where finally they said their last prayers before passing over to a better life. It is a beautiful example of the 18th. century mannerist style.

Barroque, with an image of Our Lady of Dolours and some crown caots of arms in stone. its columns are formed of stone figures also, they represent the hanged ones with their disfigured and fiendish semblances and their deformed faces and bodies.

Not very far from there you have the 'Posada de las Animas' the Ghost Inn, today a home for old age pensioners; though it has been restored it goes back to 1500. The origin of its peculiar name comes from the entrance door where some shin bones and skeletons are depicted, which simbolise the end of this life, there is also a picture of Our Lady fetching some souls from purgatory. This old Inn was for drovers as well as for gentlemen (knights) who were passing through. It had the honour of Welcoming the gread writer D. Miguel de Cervantes y Saavedra, as well as many other important figures from all over Spain. There stayed a no less illustrious person than the Rondan writer D. Vicente Espinel.

– Dear friend, you are pursuading me to postpone my departure.

No Sir, I am only trying to convince you of what has been left intapped.

– I see, but I realise that you have only spoken to me of famous sons, monuments, and illustrious deeds, so, what about the ordinary people? and Rondan women?

How right you are, but you are in such a hurry!

The ordinary people, they are the begettors of all this splendour that is Ronda. As for the Rondan women I am sorry that I have not spoken of them before.

In general the Rondan woman is virtuous, religious and abounding in good qualities and was always at the side of her menfolk during the time of transcendental happenings in our town. In answer to your two questions, I tell you that the ordinary people also produced women that, through one circumstance or another are heralded in the deeds of our history.

Have you heard speak of 'Carmen of Ronda' that legendary woman on whom Bizet based his opera 'Carmen'.

During the war of Independence that woman, who was not very well thought of by the townsfolk, because they did not know quite what she did, had a great influence on the resistance to the French occupation on account of her movements and deeds. She was the one who gave warning of the dynamiting of the Alcazaba by the French, and thanks to her, it was possible to save part of it, as well as avoiding greater ills to the inhabitants of the town.

But let us continue with the ordinary people and talk about a woman whom everybody remembers with great affection. Ana Amaya Molina 'Aniya the Gypsy'; she was born in Ronda on the 27th. of September 1855, a 'great singer and dancer' (in the Andalusian style) it was said that when Aniya sang and played, the world came to an end. She was the grand aunt of the extraordinary 'artiste' Carmen Amaya who learnt many Rondan songs from her. She sang and played all over Spain, in the most reknowned places and with the best singers of that time. The queen Vitoria Eugenia made her a gift of a 'manton de manila', after having performed at an intimate gathering for the royal family.

Loved and respected by everyne she was acquainted with artists and poets from García Lorca to Manuel de Falla, the name of Aniya the gypsy was on all their lips as a key figure of famous songs and songs from the Serranía.

But others of course, were to blame for deeds that were not quite praiseworthy, because of course, all sorts inhabit the Lord's vineyard.

Listen I am going to tell you the story of a Rondan man, a little legendary, whose wife was the cause of his ending his life outsede the law. This man was José Ulloa, a member of the team of Pedro Romero (the bullfighter) very skilled in the Rondan art of bullfighting. This man was married to a gypsy from Ronda, she was called Nena, also a dancer, he was delirious about her. One day when the war of Independence was over a bullfight was organised in Málaga, it was to celebrate the arrival of Ferdinand VII 'The desired one, back to Spain, and his services were required as second swordsman. Near the little town of El Burgo he fell from his horse, breaking an arm. Realising that there was no point in continuing he decided to return to Ronda. Arriving there rather late at night, he noticed that his wife was a little nervous and restless. Our friend became suspicious and began to search the house until he found, in a huge oil jar, the sexton of the neighbouring parish. He killed them both and fled to the Sierra.

Not long afterwards he appeared as a member af the famous gang 'The seven youngsters of Ecija' and even though this gang was eventually brought to justice, Tragabuches remained in the Sierra until in time he disappeared without leaving a trace.

What he did leave behind him was a little rime, which has always been sung by the people of the Sierra and goes like this: 'A woman was the cause of my downfall, there is no perdition of man that doesn't originate from a woman'.

– Tell me, referring to Bandoleros, there must be many stories referring to them?

Many and interesting one that would give you a clearer idea of the situation in our Serranía at that time and above all of the character of our Serrano people.

But friend, as you are in a hurry and you intend to return, because everyone returns to Ronda, I promise to tell you about them and continue to enjoy your company.

You must use your afternoon in seeing Acinipo and the Caves de la Pileta.

In order to visit them both you must go along the Sevilla road. At about 5 km. from Ronda you will find a crossroads which will take you to Acinipo (Ronda la Vieja); but if you continue on the Sevilla road to about 12 kms. to the left you will see a sign to the Cueva de la Pileta; on leaving Ronda by this same road, there is a branch road with a sign to Benaojan, take it and you will soon get to the cave.

The road to Ronda la Vieja will take you to Acinipo; if you continue it will take you to the wonderful village of Setenil de las Bodegas.

Acinipo is situated at about 800 metres above sea level, in the heart of Roman Andalucia. Pliny and Ptolomy placed it in the celtic region Beturia, it became a municipality with rights for minting money until it was destroyed by the vandals in 429.

Time has been much more generous than the vandals for it has proudly preserved the ruins of its theatre.

When you arrive you can admire, from the road the stage wall built with big stones. Much nearer and viewing it from the stone seats you will see that it has three doors and above them niches for placing either statues of gods or tribunes.

Recently the rooms used by the actors have been discovered and also the place for the musicians, the stage and the space between the stage and the auditorium. here you can see the remains of large red marble flagstones which covered the floor of the theatre.

Also the seating has been uncovered. You can see that the majority of them are worked in stone, as in Greek theatres, using the uneveness of the ground some stairways give access to the upper and lower seating.

The panoramic views are wonderful and around the theatre you will still see the remains of stones and tiles and the remains of houses and buildings which will help you to understand the barberous state of destruction to which the town was subject. But above all at the entrance you will find some very important foundations dating from a former Iberian township.

Some vertical stones will show even today the original limits of the town.

Finally return to the Sevilla road and follow it until you see the sign which will leave you at the very door of the Cueva de la Pileta.

You will go through such picturesque villages that they will look more like white spots in the Serrania (mountains). These villages are Montejaque and Benaojan, of Arab origen, hardworking, pretty, clean, friendly and proud of their land as nowhere else in Spain.

If you should stop in either of them you can visit one of the many factories which turn out pork products of well merited fame from our Serrania. You will also see how well the inhabitants look after their villages and keep them clean like the true gems that they are.

We have in our Serrania numerous caves of extraordinary value from the speleological and historic point of view. Besides the Cueva de la Pileta, we should also mention one called cueva del Gato (the Cat's Cave) near the railway station of Benaoján-Montejaque, which even today has not been totally discovered and where a few years ago a Valencian speleologist lost his life.

The Cueva de la Pileta was discovered in 1905 by D. Jose Bullon Lobato. Later in 1911 it was visited by the English colonel Mr. Vernet who through several publications in the English press, made it known to the world. Following on this, two experts Mr. Breuil and Mr. Obermaier studied and spoke of its prehistoric value.

It was declared an national monument in 1924. When you see it you will feel the immense pleasure of the beauty of nature harmonising so well with beauty created by man who lived here for thousands of years.

Traversing majestic chambers or narrow passages and galleries you will find wonderful shapes formed by nature and matching the stalactites and stalagmites. You will find chambers such as the Bat's chamber, that of the serpents, the castle, the Moorish queen, the cathedral, the dead woman, the fish, the waterfall, the great abyss, the organ, the sanctuary, etc.:

Numerous ceramic remains and utensils from Paleolithic and Neolithic times have been found, some can be seen in the cave; others are in museums in different parts of Spain. You will see the skeleton of a young woman that in the course of time has become petrified.

You can also admire rupestral paintings of incalculable value in ochre, yellow or black; some of these in red or yellow dating from 15.000 years ago.

There are numerous signs and diagrams which are clearly magical-religious. But from this prehistoric pantheon I wish to emphasise the Sanctuary Chamber of The Fish.

The Sanctuary is the most outstanding part of the cavern, for its perfect paintings. Apart from two human figures and countless signs, there are fourteen paleolithic representations, probably Solutrense where a pregnant mare is the most representative, the Fish Chamber is no less important as it is the most spectacular of the whole visit. It is large with many black diagrammatic emblems from Neolithic times, and where the most emblematic drawing in the cave is to be encountered "THE FISH" 150 cms. long and 80 cms. wide. It is black, painted with vegetal charcoal; it is the most significant paleolithic painting in this prehistoric sanctuary. There are many paintings of animals of the surrounding area and of its epoch.

After walking for miles in the interior of the cave, you will re-emerge, contemplate the landscape which surrounds you and you will think; How wise is nature and how great the hand of God who concentrated so much beauty in so few kilometres of our Serrania.

Before we part, I would like to hear from you travellers, visitors, writers, painters, and sensitive spirits, who praised and popularised every corner of the world that you have known and visited, you have also visited one of the places most favoured by nature and history where your contact and observation open up areas of serenity and exclamation, of wonder and peacefulness.

So, dear friend the list of people having known the beautiful queen and have not dedicated at least one thought, one compliment, or a few beautiful words, would be long, very long; but let us mention a few as samples, Juan Ramón Jiménez says "Ronda, high and deep, full and profound, round and elevated." or Antonio Gala, "Like a furtive whisper". or Rafael Alberti who dedicates to her "The merry jokes of the lad from La Palma". or Eugenio Dors in his motives from Andalucia which encourage him to visit it. "The Mute Cicerone". or Federico Garcia Lorca in his "Mariana Pineda" scene IV, stanza I. Gerardo Diego "The emplacement of Ronda". Dionisio Ridruejo "An Afternoon Stroll". José María Pemán "Ronda and the poet". And the no less world figures, such as James Joyce who dedicates to Ronda the final part of his great work "Ulysses" or Prospero Merimée who creates Carmen from a Ronda girl or Rainer María Rilke in a dream spirit in his Spanish Trilogy "or" Collected Letters". Ernest Hemingway in everything that he wrote about Spain, he also had a thouught for our beloved city, "Death in the Afternoon". Richard Ford, Reniero Dozy, David Robert, Gustave Dore, etc:.., and one last memory for that very versatile person who decided, after wandering around and getting to know the world to have his ashes scatterd over the place where beauty is nature. "Orson Welles".

Here, since our visit is finished. Good day and a happy journey.

⇧
⇧ Cayetano Ordóñez "Niño de la Palma". Ernest Hemingway y
    Antonio Ordóñez. 1959.   Foto Miguel Mar█
⇧ Orson Welles and Antonio Ordóñez - 1964   Foto Salvador Ordóñez "Cus

EPILOGUE

Having finished this new work, in which I continue with dialogues and text from my former book, because I have been told that its success was due to its familiar style but I find that I have missed several voids and lacunae, which troubled me deeply.

When I reread my manuscripts, and the more I reread them the more I felt like tearing them up and beginning them anew. But then I asked myself: who is going to read them if I delve too much? How am I to interest those hundreds of thonsands of visitors who every day discover the town of Ronda? Where could I get the help which would lead me into an in depth publication?

We live in a society whore time is limited, although time is eternal, where convenience directs us towards interests alien to reality, and towards which we find ourselves directed and manipulated by forces with different aims, rather than by rational sense.

I only hope that you who have this book in your hand will use it to discover The Beautiful Mystery and that it may serve as an introduction to it, and that your sensitivity and greatness of spirit will encourage you to discover this Enchanted City. That you may stroll with your eyes open and that you may not be dazzled with dreams like many inhabitants of Ronda, may this litte volume accomplished with much love and suffering help you to know that God is lavish and also remote, with this Dream City of Dreams where the "Mute Guide" will encourage you to become deeply acquainted with it, to come into contact with its corners and shadows, its doors and grills, with its streets and squares, because sensitive souls, wanderers from other regions, remote from Ronda will rest their weary limbs in the shade of Wadi-al-Laban and its history.

THE AUTHOR

INDEX

Prologue 5
Introduction 7
A brief history 11
The visit 37
New Bridge 37
Plane Nº 1 40
Santo Domingo Convet 41
House of the Counts of Santa Pola 41
Old Bridge 42
House of the Moorish King 42
Mercadillo 44
Church of Padre Jesús 45
Convent of the Mother of God 46
Arab Baths 46
Plane Nº 2 48
Walls and the Gare of Xijara 65
Palace of the Marquis of Salvatierra 66
Minaret of San Sebastián 66
Duchess of Parcent square 67
Plane Nº 3 68
The Castle and Town Hall 70
Santa María la Mayor 71
Mondragón Palace - Municipal Archeological Museum 74
Plane Nº 4 78
The Church of la Virgen de la Paz - Giant's House 75
Bullring 76
Park and Carmelite Convent 80
Plane Nº 5 100
San Francisco Quarter and Almocábar gate 101
The Church of the Holy Spirit 101
Illustrious Citizens 102
Acinipo 106
Cave of la Pileta 107
Epilogue 111

Palacio Mondragón

Palacio Mondragón
Patio siglo XVIII

↑ Patio Mudéjar - Palacio Mondragón - Patio siglo XVIII ⇓

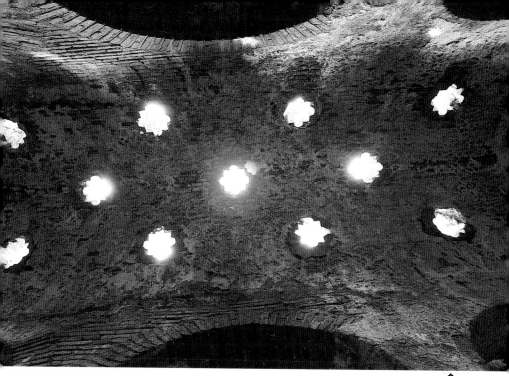

Baños Arabes - Arabien Baths - Bagni Arabi - Bains Arabes- Dampfbäder

Vistas aéreas. Aerial views. Vues aeriennes. Vedute Aeree. Luftaussichten

⇧ Baños Arabes   ⇩ Cueva de la Pileta

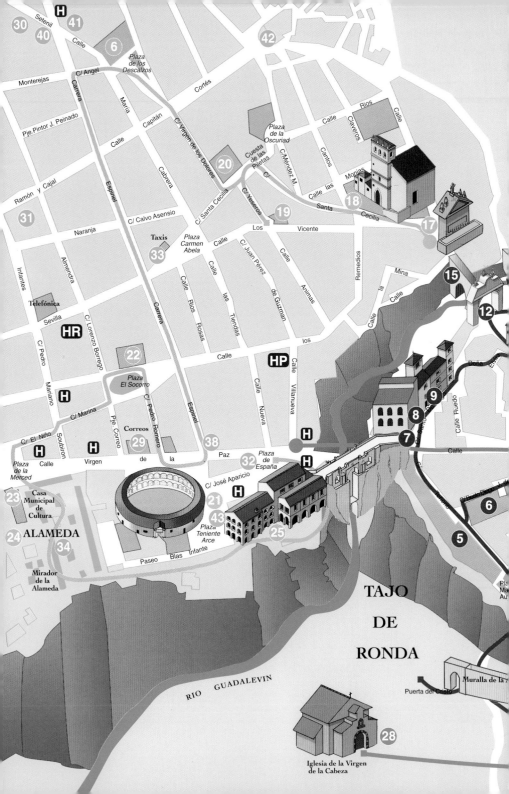

MONUMENTS

ITINERARY 1: ▬▬

1. Church of our Lady of the Incarnation.
2. City Hall.
3. Convent of St. Isabel of the Angels.
4. Mondragón Palace.
5. House of Saint John Bosco.
6. Church of Our Lady of Peace.
7. The New Bridge.
8. Convent of Santo Domingo.
9. House of the Moorish King.
10. Minaret of San Sebastián.
11. Palace of the Marquis of Salvatierra.
12. Gate of Philip V.
13. Bridge of San Miguel.
14. Arab Baths.
15. Old Bridge or Arabian Bridge.
16. Ramparts of Xijara.

ITINERARY 2: ▬▬

17. Fountain of Eight Spouts.
18. Parish of Padre Jesús.
19. Inn of Our Lady of Souls.
20. Chapel of Our Lady of Sorrows.
21. Bullring.
22. Church of Socorro.
23. Convent of La Merced.
24. Alameda-Promenade of the Gorge
25. Parador.

ITINERARY 3: ▬▬

26. The Holy Spirit Church.
27. Ramparts of Almocabar and Gates of Almocabar.
28. Rupestrian Church of Virgen de la Cabeza.
A. Giants Museum.

29. Post Office.
30. Rail Road Station.
31. Bus Terminal.
32. Tourist Office
33. Taxis.
34. Theatre.
35. Bandit Museum.
36. Archaelogical Museum.
37. Peinado Museum.
38. Main Street.
39. Local Police.
40. National Police.
41. Civil Guard.
42. Hospital.
43. Local Tourist Office.

RONDA ©